Don't Tell the Teacher

Gervase Phinn is a teacher, freelance lecturer, author, poet, educational consultant, school inspector, visiting professor of education and, last but by no means least, father of four. Most of his time is spent in schools with teachers and children.

He is the author of the bestselling books for adults *The Other Side of the Dale*, *Over Hill and Dale*, *Head Over Heels in the Dales* and *Up and Down in the Dales*, three volumes of children's poetry and three fiction books for young children.

Gervase Phinn

Don't Tell the Teacher

Illustrated by Chris Mould

PUFFIN

'So There!' on page 53 is taken from

Up and Down the Dales (Michael Joseph, 2004).

PUFFIN BOOKS

Published by the Penguin Group
Penguin Books Ltd, 80 Strand, London WC2R 0RL, England
Penguin Group (USA) Inc., 375 Hudson Street, New York, New York 10014, USA
Penguin Group (Canada), 90 Eglinton Avenue East, Suite 700, Toronto, Ontario, Canada M4P 2Y3
(a division of Pearson Penguin Canada Inc.)
Penguin Ireland, 25 St Stephen's Green, Dublin 2, Ireland (a division of Penguin Books Ltd)
Penguin Group (Australia), 250 Camberwell Road, Camberwell, Victoria 3124, Australia
(a division of Pearson Australia Group Pty Ltd)
Penguin Books India Pvt Ltd, 11 Community Centre, Panchsheel Park, New Delhi - 110 017, India
Penguin Group (NZ), cnr Airborne and Rosedale Roads, Albany, Auckland 1310, New Zealand
(a division of Pearson New Zealand Ltd)
Penguin Books (South Africa) (Pty) Ltd, 24 Sturdee Avenue, Rosebank, Johannesburg 2196, South Africa

Penguin Books Ltd, Registered Offices: 80 Strand, London WC2R 0RL, England

penguin.com

First published 2006

1

Text copyright © Gervase Phinn, 2006
Illustrations copyright © Chris Mould, 2006
All rights reserved

The moral right of the author and illustrator has been asserted

Set in 12/16 Joanna
Made and printed in England by Clays Ltd, St Ives plc

British Library Cataloguing in Publication Data
A CIP catalogue record for this book is available from the British Library

ISBN-13: 978-0-141-32074-8
ISBN-10: 0-141-32074-5

For Nina and Richard

Contents

Early Sighting

Matthew saw a grey squirrel,
Poking a curious face
Though the branches of the tree,
Which stood outside the classroom window.
'Look!' he said to Andrew,
'Let's tell the teacher.'
'Don't you say a word,' replied his friend.
'She'll have us write about it!'

Supply Teacher

Dear Mrs Auchterloonie,
I'm writing just to say,
That I'm really really sorry
That you are still away.

The supply teacher has told us
That we have to write this letter,
Hoping that you're on the mend
And that you'll soon be better.

Our new teacher's called Miss Merriman
And she used to teach my mum,
And although she's pretty old now,
She's such a lot of fun.

She reads us super stories
And we paint and draw and sing,
And she's brilliant at outdoor games –
In fact, she's great at everything.

I've got really good at number work
Since Miss Merriman showed me how,
And my writing's so much neater
And my reading's better now.

Miss Merriman's put our work up
All down the corridor.
The headteacher says he's never seen
A display as good before.

We do poetry and pottery
And spellings on a Friday.
Oh, and she's reorganized your storeroom
Because Miss Merriman likes things tidy.

She's packed up the computers,
And the pictures from the wall,
And taken all your potted plants
And put them in the hall.

She's emptied all your drawers out,
And put things in a tin.
And she's collected all our workbooks
And put them in the bin.

She's moved around the tables
And the chairs, she's rearranged.
You wouldn't recognize our classroom
Because everything has changed.

Miss Merriman is fantastic.
I think she's really cool.
Well, I hope my letter's cheered you up
And you'll soon be back at school.

My Best Friend

My best friend:

Sat next to David in class instead of **me**,
Talked about **me** behind my back,
Wrote things about **me** on the wall,
Got **me** into trouble with Miss,
Never asked **me** to his party,
Wouldn't look **me** in the eye,
Told **me** I was boring,
Said he didn't like **me** any more.
'The trouble is with you,' he told **me**,
'It's always **me**, **me**, **me**, **me**, **me**!'

A Close Companion

As you sit all tense in the dentist's chair,
Eyes tightly closed, hands pressed together,
Listening to the whining drill –
I am there,
With you.

As you lie in bed in the shadowy dark,
And outside a cold wind rustles the leaves,
And branches scrape the window like claws –
I am there,
With you.

As you wade in the warm blue water,
Feeling the sandy sea bed soft beneath your feet,
And imagining what creature swims below –
I am there,
With you.

As you prepare to tell the angry teacher,
Who sits glowering at his desk,
That you have not done your homework –
I am there,
With you.

I am the one who
Makes you tremble and sweat,
Makes your heart beat like a drum,
Makes your throat dry and your chest tight,
I am the one who fills your head with the most dreadful
thoughts –
And you know my name.

Bully

Bully –
Cold eyes.
Hits me hard,
Calls me cruel names.
My friend says,
'Ignore him.'
How?

School Inspector

Inspector –
Cold eyes,
Sharp white teeth,
Smiles like a crocodile,
Frightens the teacher,
Who stands,
Trembling.

Dad and the Dog

'It's your turn to take the dog for a walk,' said Dad to Lizzie.

'No, it isn't. I took him on Monday.'

'It's your turn to take the dog for a walk,' said Dad to Dominic.

'No, it isn't. I took him on Tuesday.'

'It's your turn to take the dog for a walk,' said Dad to Matthew.

'No, it isn't. I took him on Wednesday.'

'It's your turn to take the dog for a walk,' said Dad to Richard.

'No, it isn't. I took him on Thursday.'

'It's your turn to take the dog for a walk,' said Dad to Mum.

'No, it isn't. I took him on Friday.'

'It must be my turn, then,' said Dad, reaching for the lead.

'Come on, Shadow. Walkies!'

But the dog was fast asleep.

He had got tired of waiting.

You Are Not Going Out Like That!

'You are not going out like that tonight!
No, you are not going out like that!
Your skirt's too short,
Your blouse too tight,
Your lips too red,
Your shoes too bright,
Your hair too wild,
You look a sight.
You are not going out like that tonight!
No, you are not going out like that!'

'Oh, don't be so old-fashioned,
Don't be such a nag.
You really are a misery-guts,
You really are a drag.
Cheer up, don't be downhearted –
You look so sad and glum.
Just remember you are my daughter, dear,
And I'm your trendy mum.'

Late Home

Mum: And where have you been until this time?

Boy: I was . . .

Mum: Playing football, I bet.

Boy: No, I was . . .

Mum: When you should have come straight home.

Boy: If I could explain . . .

Mum: The times I tell you . . .

Boy: You see, I was . . .

Mum: To come straight home.

Boy: But . . .

Mum: You just don't listen, do you?

Boy: I do, but . . .

Mum: In one ear and out the other.

Boy: But . . .

Mum: No more buts, young man.

Boy: You see . . .

Mum: Now, go and wash your hands.

Boy: I'm trying to tell you . . .

Mum: Tea will be on the table in five minutes.

Boy: The thing is . . .

Mum: Have you any homework?

Boy: Yes, I have, but . . .

Mum: Well, after tea it's up to your room.

Boy: Could I explain . . .

Mum: And no television tonight.

Boy: I'm trying to tell you . . .

Mum: Don't just stand there.

Boy: Will you listen, please?

Mum: Do as you're told!

Boy: Mrs Wilson!!!!!

Mum: Pardon?

Boy: I've been trying to tell you!

Mum: What?

Boy: That I am not your son and you're not my mum.

Mum: Oh!

Boy: I live next door.

School Trip

The great green shiny monster stands still,
Buffed and burnished,
A cold exhibit in a vast museum.
Never again will it rattle down the rails,
Hissing steam, belching smoke,
Clacking and clattering on the track,
Its whistle shrieking.
But there is still the far-off smell of oil and coke –
A slight reminder of when the monster lived and breathed.

'Come along, daydreamer,' says my teacher,
'Your worksheet's incomplete.'
And so I count the rivets on the engine
And estimate the length of a carriage.

Dream On

I'm a daydreamer, a daydreamer,
Head in the clouds all day.
I'm a daydreamer, a daydreamer,
Dreaming my life away.

My brother's in a pop group,
My mum's a movie star,
My uncle's a world champion
And drives a racing car.

My sister is a model
And my dad's a millionaire,
And we all live in this castle –
And I do not have a care.

I'm a daydreamer, a daydreamer,
Head in the clouds all day.
I'm a daydreamer, a daydreamer,
Dreaming my life away.

My brother's in no pop group,
In fact, he hasn't a guitar.
My uncle's not world champion,
He doesn't own a car.

My sister's not a model,
Nor my dad a millionaire,
But I do live in a castle –
It's a castle in the air.

I'm a daydreamer, a daydreamer,
Head in the clouds all day.
I'm a daydreamer, a daydreamer,
Dreaming my life away.

For when I dream, I leave behind
A mum who doesn't care,
A brother who's a bully,
And a dad who's never there.

For when I dream, I leave behind
A life that's bleak and bare,
And I live inside my castle –
My castle in the air.

I'm a daydreamer, a daydreamer,
Head in the clouds all day.
I'm a daydreamer, a daydreamer,
Dreaming my life away.

A Trip to the Zoo

Please, don't bring me back to the zoo,
No, don't bring me back to the zoo.
The trumpeting elephant looks really mad,
The old hippopotamus dreadfully sad,
As I said to my mum and I said to my dad,
Please, don't bring me back to the zoo.

Please, don't bring me back to the zoo,
No, don't bring me back to the zoo.
The bored-looking tiger gnaws on a bone,
The poor old gorilla sits all on his own,
As I said to my parents, oh, can I go home?
Please, don't bring me back to the zoo.

Please, don't bring me back to the zoo,
No, don't bring me back to the zoo.
The chimps in their cages look terribly glum,
The wolves in their pens have nowhere to run,
As I said to my dad and I said to my mum,
Please, don't bring me back to the zoo.

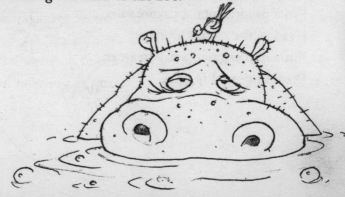

Who Said What

To the boy with his head
Stuck through the railings in the park,

The Optimist said:	Don't worry, son, we'll soon have you out.
The Psychiatrist said:	How do you feel?
The Photographer said:	Smile please!
The Counsellor said:	Would you care to talk about it?
The Pessimist said:	You might never get out.
The Blacksmith said:	Nice piece of ironwork.
The Traffic Warden said:	You can't stay there.
The Sympathizer said:	I know just how you feel.
The Stoic said:	Just grin and bear it.
The Clairvoyant said:	I thought this might happen.
The Newspaper Reporter said:	HEADLINE – BOY IN PARK RAILING ORDEAL!
The Philosopher said:	It's merely a state of mind.
The Job's Comforter said:	You've probably damaged your neck.
The Joker said:	Don't go away.
The Realist said:	You've got your head stuck.

But the boy with his head
Stuck through the railings in the park said simply:
  GET ME OUT!

A Letter from Lizzie

Dear Granny and Grandpa,

Mother's come out in a rash,
Father's got the mumps,
Richard's got a tummy ache,
Dominic's got lumps.
Matthew's got German measles,
But there's nothing wrong with me,
And I cannot wait for Sunday,
When you're coming round for tea.

Grandpa

Anne's grandpa wears glasses,
Bimla's grandpa's deaf,
Colin's has a walking stick and gets really out of breath,
Donna's grandpa's small and thin,
Eric's has got a cat,
Freddie's grandpa wears big boots and a shapeless woollen hat,
Guy's grandpa wears yellow socks,
Harry's, he wears red,
Ian's gramp's called Sidney and likes to stay in bed,
Jay's grandpa likes bingo,
Kirit's likes the telly,
Leroy's, he wears aftershave that's really really smelly,
Malika's grandpa's wrinkled,
Nuala's smokes cigars,
Olive's wears a ginger wig and likes to drive fast cars,
Paul's grandpa does crosswords,
Quentin's rides a bike,
Ronnie's sits in the park all day and smokes a massive pipe,
Sammy's grandpa's very old,
Tamsin's grandpa's young,
Una's, he goes fishing and he's only got one lung,
Veronica's grandpa's grumpy,
William's laughs a lot,
Xavier's is really rich and owns a giant yacht.
Yvonne's grandfather's just retired, he used to drive a train,
Zoe never sees her gramps, because he lives in Spain.

But my grandpa, he is different,
He's not like any other.
He's not like my dad's dad at all,
He's more like my big brother.
He wears designer trainers,
And all the latest clothes,
And he's dyed his hair bright yellow,
And has five studs in his nose.
He goes to all the discos,
And dances until morn,
But then is out there jogging,
At the very crack of dawn.
He has tattoos along his arms,
And a ring though both his ears,
And if you say, 'Good morning,'
He always answers, 'Cheers!'
He makes my mother angry,
My dad fly in a rage,
You see, my grandpa's seventy-five –
But he doesn't act his age!

New Kid

There's a new kid
In our class,
Fast as lightning,
Bold as brass,
Cool as a cucumber,
Fierce as a lion,
Strong as a horse,
Hard as iron,
Fit as a fiddle,
Tall as a tree,
Broad as a barn door,
Rough as can be.
I hope that she'll be friends with me.

Home

In the Home Corner,
In an infant school classroom,
A boy and girl,
Rising five,
Were arguing,
Stabbing the air with small fingers,
Jutting out their chins,
And stamping little feet.
'Oh, do shut up!'
'No, you shut up!'
'I'm sick of you!'
'I'm sick of you!'
'Oh, just be quiet!'
'No, you be quiet!'
'Oh, do shut up!'
'No, you shut up!'
'What is all this?' the teacher cried.
'We're playing mums and dads,'
The infants both replied.

Down Menagerie Street

Mrs Moore,
Who lives next door,
Owns a red and blue macaw.

Mr Joad,
Across the road,
Has a green and yellow toad.

Miss O'Mally,
Down the alley,
Calls her furry rabbit Sally.

Sir Titus Pain,
In the lane,
Keeps a bulldog on a chain.

Old Miss Black,
On the cul-de-sac,
Has a duck which doesn't quack.

Dr Platts,
In the flats,
Lives with two grey Siamese cats.

Mrs Gerard,
On the boulevard,
Keeps a donkey in her yard.

Professor Clive,
Down the drive,
Keeps buzzing bees in a hive.

Lady Low,
On the row,
Has a tame but noisy crow.

Reverend Fleet,
Down the street,
Has a talking parakeet.

Dear Miss Pleasant,
On the crescent,
In her garden has a pheasant.

Lord St Clair,
By the thoroughfare,
In his stable keeps a mare.

But there's a house that's cold and stark.
It's through the wood, beyond the park,
And there lives Mr and Mrs Clark,
Who have a pond that's deep and dark
And their pet is – a great white shark!

Teacher's Pet

Miss Perkins has a vulture.
It perches on her chair
And watches all the children,
As quietly they sit there.

Its feathers are a battleship grey,
Bright yellow are its claws,
Its beak is as sharp as razor blades
And its wings like giant oars.

Miss Perkins has no problems
With naughty girls and boys.
Her class is always well behaved
And never makes a noise.

The children sit in silence,
They never speak a word,
They never walk about the room,
When Miss Perkins brings the bird.

No one even whispers,
No one scrapes a chair,
No one moves a muscle,
When the teacher's pet is there.

Art Lesson

'Your picture's most unusual,' Miss Moore, our teacher, said,
'But I've never seen a porcupine with horns upon its head,
And lavender lions and silver snakes and a cow in a
    crimson coat,
Nor have I seen an orange mouse or a rainbow-coloured
    goat.
And what is this, a crocodile, with a gold ring through its
    nose?
A purple bat, a spotted rat and a parrot wearing clothes?
I can't recall that I have ever seen a monkey in a hat,
A camel sporting spectacles or a multicoloured cat.
Oh dearie me, a chimpanzee, flying in a plane,
A grizzly bear with yellow hair and a pig with a purple mane.
And what is this you've painted here – a hive of scarlet bees,
A turtle playing tiddlywinks and an elephant on skis.
Now, sit right down and please don't frown,' our teacher
    duly sighed,
'And pick your paintbrush up again and have another try.'

Up and Down

Up and down, up and down, on the escalator in the town,
Up **and** down, up and down, on the escalator in the town,
Up and **down**, up and down, on the escalator in the town,
Up and down, **up** and down, on the escalator in the town,
Up and down, up **and** down, on the escalator in the town,
Up and down, up and **down**, on the escalator in the town,
Up and down, up and down, **on** the escalator in the town,
Up and down, up and down, on **the** escalator in the town,
Up and down, up and down, on the **escalator** in the town,
Up and down, up and down, on the escalator **in** the town,
Up and down, up and down, on the escalator in **the** town,
Up and down, up and down, on the escalator in the **town**.

The Carousel

Little Lizzie felt quite dizzy
On the circus carousel.
Round and round and up and down,
You should have heard poor Lizzie yell.
'I do not like it! Do not like it!'
Everyone heard Lizzie shout.
'It's making me feel really queasy,
Will you stop this roundabout?'

Round and round and up and down,
And up and down and round and round.
'I do not like this horrid ride,
I want my feet on solid ground.'
But when the carousel was over,
Little Lizzie said, 'You know,
I found the experience quite exciting.
I think I'd like another go.'

Dominic's Discovery

She secretes them in spaghetti,
Hides them under chips,
Camouflages them in pizza,
Buries them in dips.
She wraps them up in batter,
Conceals them in baked beans,
Envelops them in gravy,
Disperses them in greens.
She chops them up with onions,
Sprinkles them with cheese,
Mashes them with cabbage,
Scatters them in peas.
She covers them in ketchup,
Submerges them in stew,
But he can still taste mushrooms
Whatever Mum tries to do.

Question

'What is the point,' asked Dad,
'Of having a stud through your tongue?'

'If you mutht know,' replied his daughter, 'I'm
exthprething my perthonality.'

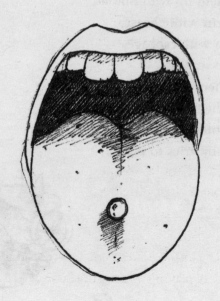

In a Dark Dark Town

In a dark dark town,
There was a dark dark street,
And in the dark dark street,
There was a dark dark school,
And in the dark dark school,
There were some dark dark gates,
And behind the dark dark gates,
There was a dark dark door,
And beyond the dark dark door,
There was a dark dark corridor,
And down the dark dark corridor,
There was a dark dark classroom,
And in the dark dark classroom,
There was a dark dark desk,
And in the dark dark desk,
There was a dark dark drawer,
And in the dark dark drawer,
There was a dark dark box,
And in the dark dark box,
There was . . .
Colin Cooper's conker, which Miss Cawthorne had confiscated
Because he was playing with it in class.

Colin's Conkers!

Miss Cawthorne says I can't play conkers any more.
She says it's far too dangerous,
Especially in class.
That I could get a bit of conker in my eye
And have to go to hospital
And that I might lose my sight.
'Conkers are banned!' she said.
I told her that I wear glasses,
So there's not much chance
Of getting a bit of conker in my eye.
Miss Cawthorne sent me to the head teacher for being cheeky.

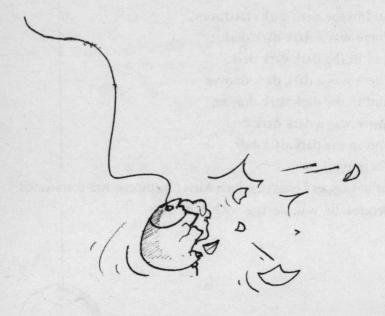

Communication

When I threw a lump of mud at Michael Morrison,
I told Miss Shoolbred I was trying to attract his attention
And I didn't mean it to land on his head.
Miss Shoolbred said there were better ways to attract his
    attention
Than throwing a lump of mud at him.
She made me stay in at playtime and think about other ways
Of communicating with people.
She told me to write them down.
And so I wrote,
'You could send them a:
    letter,
    note,
    postcard,
    fax,
    email or
    Morse code message.
You could:
    phone them up or
    send them a smoke signal.'
Miss Shoolbred sent me to the head teacher
To communicate with him.

Leroy's Laugh

When Leroy laughed
The whole class started laughing.
It was a huffing, puffing,
Guffawing, hee-hawing,
Braying, neighing,
Thundering, ear-splitting sort of a laugh.
'Not so loud, Leroy,' said the teacher,
'It's enough to wake the dead.'
Then Leroy left.
Oh, how we missed his laugh.
Our classroom now seems as silent as the grave.

Infant Nativity Play

Mary in a pale blue cloak,
Joseph with a towel over his head,
Held in place by an elastic belt with snake clasp,
Approached the cardboard inn
And knocked.

'Have you a room?' asked Joseph.
'Sorry,' said the innkeeper, shaking his little head.
'But we have travelled far,' said Joseph.
'No room at the inn.'
'And we are tired, very tired.'
'We are all full up and have no room.'
'And my dear wife is to have a baby.'
'We have no room at the inn,' said the innkeeper.
'Oh, please,' begged Joseph, 'just for the night.'

The innkeeper,
In a pale brown dressing gown
And bright red slippers,
Observed the little travellers,
Sad and weary and far from home,
And scratched his head.
'Have my room,' he said, smiling,
'And I'll sleep in the stable.'

Celebration

I really am excited!
We're having a bit of a celebration
In our house tonight.
Mum said that when Dad sees my school report
There will be fireworks!

REPORT

Driving

My father drives an ambulance,
My mother drives a van,
My sister drives a sports car
And my brother drives a tram,
My uncle drives a forklift truck,
My auntie drives a cab,
But they all agree, when it comes to me,
I simply drive them mad!

In the Bathroom

'Will you come out of the bathroom!
You've been in nearly half an hour.
I need to pay a visit,
I need to take a shower,
I need to give my teeth a clean,
I need to wash my hair,
Every morning it's always the same,
What on earth do you do in there?'

'I can't come out of the bathroom!
If I tell you, please don't laugh.
I've got my toe stuck up the tap
While soaking in the bath.'

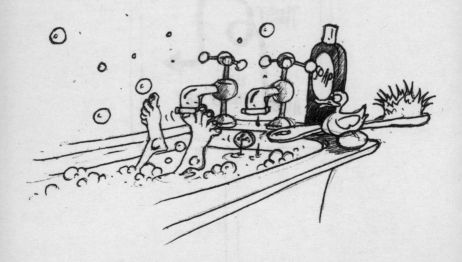

Speech Day

'And the prize for the best attendance this year goes to
   William Webster.
(Silence)
To William Webster.
(Silence)
Is William Webster here?'
'No, sir. He hasn't turned up!'

Creative Writing

My story on Monday began:
> Mountainous seas crashed on the cliffs,
> And the desolate land grew wetter . . .

The teacher wrote a little note:
> Remember the capital letter!

My story on Tuesday began:
> Red tongues of fire licked higher and higher
> From Etna's smoking top . . .

The teacher wrote a little note:
> Where is your full stop?

My story on Wednesday began:
> Through the dark, pine-scented woods
> There twists a hidden path . . .

The teacher wrote a little note:
> Start a paragraph!

My story on Thursday began:
> The trembling child, eyes dark and wild,
> Frozen midst the fighting . . .

The teacher wrote a little note:
> Take care, untidy writing!

My story on Friday began:
    The boxer bruised and bloody lay,
    His eyes half-closed and swollen . . .
The teacher wrote a little note:
    Use a semicolon!

Next Monday my story will begin:
    Once upon a time . . .

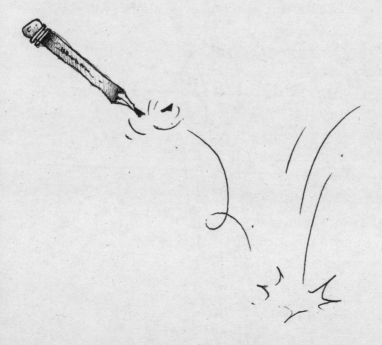

New Boy

When we had PE,
The new boy changed in the toilets,
Out of sight of all the others.
'Shy, are we?' asked the teacher impatiently,
When the boy emerged in grubby shirt and shorts.
'Come along, son, let's have that top off.
You cannot do PE wrapped up like that.'
'Please, sir,' pleaded the boy, 'can I keep it on?'
'You heard me!' snapped the teacher.
With downcast eyes, the new boy
Pulled the shirt slowly over his head
And we all saw the dark blue bruises on his thin white arms.

Letter to a Bully

Dear Martin,

I saw your name in the paper
The other day,
And thought I'd write.
You probably won't remember me
But I remember you.

I remember your cold blue eyes
And nasty smile,
And how you mouthed, 'You're dead!'
Across the classroom
When the teacher looked the other way.

I remember my cut lip
And bloody nose,
And how I rubbed by bruised shins
On the way home,
When you had run off laughing.

I remember the ache and hurt
And fear inside,
And how I dreaded end of school,
With you in wait outside
To push me up against the wall.

Yes, I saw your name in the paper
The other day,
And thought I'd write.
As I said, you probably won't remember me,
But, oh, how I remember you.

Henry Smails

The chief defect of Henry Smails
Was chewing at his fingernails.
Nibble, nibble all the day,
He nibbled all his nails away.
Then foolish Henry licked his lips
And started on his fingertips.
His worried parents were bereft,
For Henry had no fingers left.
Then, to his parents' deep dismay,
His hands and arms were gnawed away.
Then his body, legs and toes,
Yes, Henry nibbled all of those.
Until at last, as we had feared,
Poor Henry, he just disappeared.
Remember, children, Henry Smails
And do not bite your fingernails.

In Trouble

The boy
Outside the head teacher's room,
Eyes red with crying,
Grubby smears on his cheeks
Where he's wiped away the tears,
Waits to be seen.

He sighs
And plucks his hair nervously,
Then springs upright,
Like a puppet on pulled strings,
At the sound of the barking order:
'Come in!'

The Inspector Man

'Twas Monday and the quembling staff
Did scyre and skrimble in their shoes.
All cractious were the pupils
And the caretaker – not amused.

Beware the inspector man, my dear,
The eyes that shine, the crockatrice grin.
Beware the soft and sugary voice –
Do not be taken in.

Miss Mimsy trivvered in her room.
Long time she stood, long time she thought.
Then, hearing a smuffling from the hall,
She snatchéd up a snick of chalk.

She heard the shuckling, wheebling cry,
Then through the door the creature came.
She saw the smile and fangling teeth
And brackling eyes aflame.

But Dean had left his sports-bag out,
It sterched before him by the door,
And as the creature clumbered in,
It tripped and trumbled to the floor.

'Oh, thou hast done a worthible deed,'
Miss Mimsy told her beamish boy,
'For thou hast foiled the inspector man.'
She griggled in her joy.

'Twas Monday and the quembling staff
Did scyre and skrimble in their shoes.
All cractious were the pupils
And Miss Mimsy – most amused.

Teacher

There was an old teacher called Blewitt,
Who was clever, and oh how he knew it.
'Pay attention!' he roared.
'The work's on the board.
Take a look and then I'll go through it!'

Using Your Imagination

On Monday Miss Morrison
Said we could paint a picture
And all use our imaginations.
I drew a dragon
In a dark and dripping cave,
With yellow scaly skin
And slithery, snake-like tail,
Blue fins and bone-white horns,
Red-eyed and breathing purple flames.
But Miss Cawthorne, when she saw it, sighed and said,
'David, dear, dragons are not yellow.
They are green!'

So There!

Our English teacher, Mr Smart,
Says writing English is an art,
That we should always take great care
When spelling words like wear and where,
Witch and which and fair and fare,
Key and quay and air and heir,
Whet and wet and flair and flare,
Wring and ring and stair and stare,
Him and hymn and their and there,
Whine and wine and pear and pare,
Check and cheque and tare and tear,
Crews and cruise and hare and hair,
Meet and meat and bear and bare,
Knot and not and layer and lair,
Loot and lute and mayor and mare.

Well, frankly, sir, I just don't care!
So there!

Letter Home

Dear Mrs McNamara,
I'm writing this to say
That your son was very naughty
When he came to school today.

The bell had gone for lessons
When your Darren wandered in,
Then he talked all through assembly
And refused to sing the hymn.

He doodled on his reading book
And wouldn't work in class,
And at break he broke a window
And dropped litter on the grass.

Your son just would not eat his lunch
Despite the dinner lady's plea,
Then he hid behind the curtains
And refused to do PE.

I have to say I do not like
Your Darren's attitude.
When the head teacher had a word with him
He was very very rude.

He stamped his feet and shouted,
Then slammed the classroom door,
And screamed and shrieked and yelled and howled
All down the corridor.

Now I'm sure you will appreciate
That the situation's grave.
I think you should keep your son at home
Until he can behave.

The thought of Darren coming back
Fills everyone with dread.
After all I'm just a pupil
And he's the deputy head.

Examiner

The school examiner, Mrs Best,
Who spent her life devising tests,
At last is sadly laid to rest,
And now in heaven *she's* assessed.

Kinds of Poem

Alphabet Poem
Here the alphabet is used as the structure for a twenty-six-line poem.

Calligram
The words used in a calligram – also called concrete or shape poetry – form the shape of the topic described.

Cautionary Verse
A narrative poem which often features a disobedient child or a foolish person who, as a result of his or her actions, comes to a sticky end. It teaches a salutary lesson.

Conversation Poem
A free verse or rhyming poem in which two characters hold a conversation.

Diamont
A seven-line poem written in the shape of a diamond which contains a contrast of ideas or descriptions. It follows this pattern:

Line 1:	The topic	(1 word)
Line 2:	Describes the topic	(2 words)
Line 3:	Expresses some action	(3 words)

Line 4:	Relates to the topic	(4 words)
Line 5:	Action words about the opposite of the topic	(3 words)
Line 6:	Describes the opposite of the topic	(2 words)
Line 7:	The opposite of the topic	(1 word)

Epitaph

A short, often very simply written poem in memory of someone who has died. You can see epitaphs carved on tombstones in the churchyard.

Free Verse

A poem without rhyme.

Limerick

A short and amusing verse of five lines which follows a fixed pattern:

Line 1:	Rhymes with second and fifth lines	(8 or 9 syllables)
Line 2:	Rhymes with first and fifth lines	(8 or 9 syllables)
Line 3:	Rhymes with fourth line	(5 or 6 syllables)
Line 4:	Rhymes with third line	(5 or 6 syllables)
Line 5:	Rhymes with first and second lines	(8 or 9 syllables)

Parody

A poem which copies the structure of a well-known poem for comic effect.

Rhyming Poem

Rhyme is when two words sound alike. Sometimes poems use rhyme to get our attention or to make us listen, sometimes to create a pleasing musical effect. Rhyme also gives pattern to the verses in a poem. In most rhyming poems the rhyme appears at the end of the line. In some it occurs in the middle of the line (internal rhyme). Full rhymes occur when the words sound exactly alike (as in 'high' and 'sky'). Near or half-rhymes are when the words sound similar but are not full rhymes (as in 'mine' and 'grime').

Rhythmic Poem

All poems have rhythm – that is, a pattern of beats or sounds. Some poems have a slow and stately rhythm, others a regular singsong rhythm.

Riddle

A riddle is a word puzzle. Some riddles are one line and others are much longer; some are easy to solve and others are very difficult.

Index of First Lines

Where there's trouble, there's bound to be

Bad Becky

but you can't help loving her!

New for 2005

After all, wouldn't you prefer to hear a story about a princess-gobbling dragon than some soppy fairy tale?

Very good stories about a BAD little girl!

Three classic poetry collections.

Friendly Matches

Runner-up for the Signal Poetry Award

'Clever, funny and nostalgic, the collection is a delight, perfectly complemented by Wegner's comic illustrations' – *Sunday Times*

Please Mrs Butler

'Hilarious and poignant verses about primary-school life. A real winner' – *Guardian*

Heard it in the Playground

Winner of the Signal Poetry Award

'Ahlberg's scored again!' – *Books for Keeps*

'Every desk should hide a copy; every staffroom should own one' – *Observer*

By the bestselling author of
Artemis Fowl

The Legend of SPUD MURPHY

Will and Marty are doomed to spend their holidays in the library. If they put a foot wrong, Mrs Murphy, the legendary librarian, will use her gas-powered spud gun and they don't want that. But in Will and Marty has Spud Murphy met her match . . .?

'Outrageous humour' - *Independent*

eoincolfer.com